THE HELPING ROCK

WRITTEN BY
TANYA HOOVER

ILLUSTRATED BY
SHANNON O'TOOLE

A PROJECT OF:

Published by ACHIEVE Publishing
120 Sherbrook Street, Winnipeg, Manitoba R3C 2B4
www.achieve-publishing.com

Bulk discounts available. For details contact:
ACHIEVE Publishing
877-270-9776
info@achievecentre.com

ISBN: 978-1-988617-24-4
ISBN: 978-1-988617-25-1 (e-book)

Printed and bound in Canada
First edition, first printing

Book design by Ninth and May Design Co.

10 9 8 7 6 5 4 3 2 1

Printed on 30% PCW Recycled Paper

To Leo, Mira, and Chris. You make my world sparkle.
—T.H.

To Alex, for all your support.
—S.O.

“I can’t do it!” Lani wails. “I can’t ride with only two wheels!”

"Oh my brave girl. It's hard, but I know you'll learn in time," Mama says.

"All my friends learned forever ago. I'm the last one."

"Your friends don't have the extra challenge you do. You have to work harder at keeping your balance. Your cousin Tai loves biking. How about asking for his help?"

"No!" Lani shouts. "I don't want *anyone's* help."

“Come sit.” Mama pats the blanket beside her. “We all need help once in a while. And when we help, we share our gifts with each other.”

“Like we share birthday gifts? I want a magic wand for my birthday. Then I’ll be able to ride my bike.” Lani frowns at her scraped knee.

“A magic wand would be fun,” Mama says. “But I don’t mean presents wrapped in a box. I mean the special talents and skills that each of us has. Those are gifts too.”

"I guess they would be hard to open." Lani sighs.

"We don't open them, but we *look* for them. Like a treasure hunt. When we discover what our gifts are, we light up inside. And when we share our gifts with others, we share that light with the world."

"How do we find our gifts?" Lani asks.

"It starts by getting to know who you are, what you like to do, and what comes easily to you. Like Tai and his bike. He enjoys riding, and he's good at it. We're all good at some things, and we all have to work harder at other things. When you find what your gifts are, you can share them. Like Paco."

"Paco has gifts too?" Lani asks.

"Oh yes," Mama laughs. "Think of all the wonders that make him the special dog he is."

"Like the way he always runs after me," Lani exclaims.

"Yes! And when you feel sad and frustrated, like when you have trouble with your bike, Paco stays close until you feel better."

Lani smiles at Paco. Having Paco and Mama close by doesn't make learning to ride a bike any easier or less frustrating, but having them with her for the hard parts makes her feel better and stronger.

"Paco is helping me." Lani pets Paco.

"You're helping him too, Lani," Mama says.

"How?" Lani looks up.

"See how happy Paco looks when you pet him." Mama tucks Lani's hair behind her ear.

"I think he's smiling." Lani giggles.

“Maybe we need a reminder to give help and ask for help.” Mama picks up a sparkly rock next to the picnic blanket and places it in Lani’s hand.

"Wow! It's so pretty," Lani says. "Look at all the colors."

"It's like the world around us," Mama says. "It's filled with so many different people and so many different gifts. When we all share our gifts and help each other, the world sparkles like the rock."

Paco barks and wags his tail. Lani looks up from the rock to see her friend Ali. “Hi, Ali!” Lani says.

“Hi, Lani.” Ali’s voice is sad. “Are you ready for the spelling test tomorrow?”

“Yes, I’m ready,” Lani says. “I love spelling!”

“I don’t,” Ali says. “I always get confused when I try to spell ‘light.’ It isn’t spelled the way it sounds.”

Lani looks at her sparkly rock. Mama says that sharing her gifts and helping makes the world sparkle, just like the rock. She could help Ali! “When I keep forgetting a word, I make up a song with the letters,” Lani says.

Ali sits up straighter and turns to Lani with wide eyes. “Will you help me do that?”

Lani scrunches her brow. “Hmmm . . . okay, I’ve got it.” She sings, “L-I-G-H-T,” to a bright tune. Ali listens for a moment and joins in.

“Thanks, Lani!” Ali says with a smile. “I won’t forget now.”

Lani smiles too. A little sparkle warms her heart.

Lani picks up the sparkly rock again and holds it out to her friend. "Ali, Mama told me that when we all share our gifts and help each other, the world sparkles like this rock. It reminded me to help you with spelling. Maybe it will remind you to help someone too."

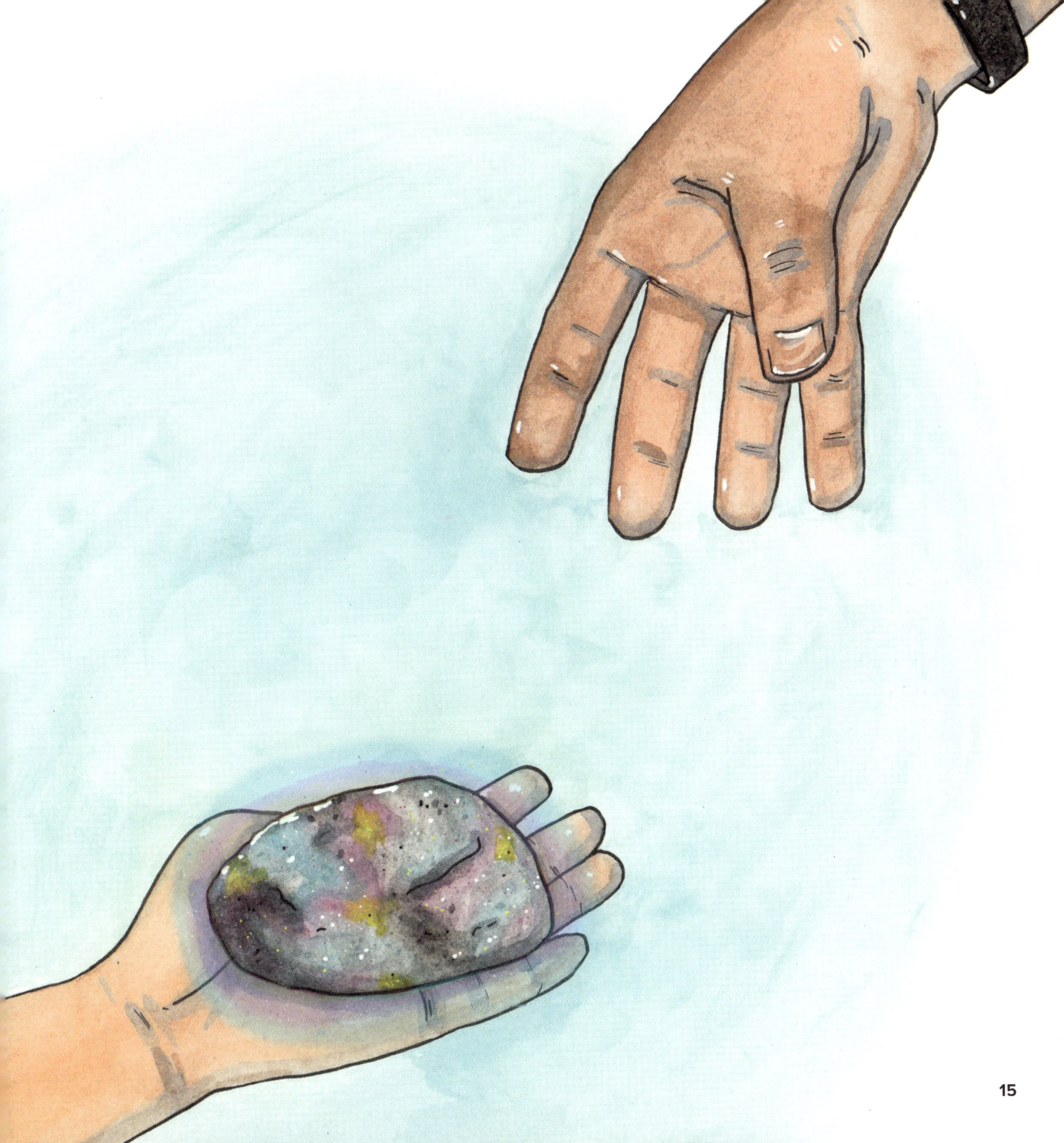

Loud voices explode. Lani and Ali look up. Their twin friends, River and Charlie, sound angry.

"Hey, what's going on?" Ali asks.

"I thought Charlie put the soccer ball in the bag." River glares at Charlie.

"I thought River put the ball in my bag." Charlie grumbles.

"Now we can't play soccer." River stomps a foot.

"Oh, that's too bad." Ali glances at the sparkly rock and then at his ball. "Hey, I'm not playing right now. Want to borrow mine?"

"Yes! Thank you!" River and Charlie say together. Ali passes the ball to them.

Ali and Lani smile at each other, and Lani nods. Ali holds the rock out to River and Charlie. “Lani helped me with spelling and then she gave me this rock to remind me to help someone else. She told me that when we all share our gifts and help each other, the world sparkles like this rock. Here, it’s your turn to have it. Maybe it will remind you too.”

"That's Jade," Lani says.
"They're shouting at Jade!"

River and Charlie catch up with Jade.

"I'm sorry they said those things to you, Jade," River says.

"Me too," Charlie adds.

River turns back to the soccer field and shouts, "We want Jade on our team."

"Yeah," Charlie says. "*Everyone* gets to play soccer."

The other players shrug and get ready for a game on the field.

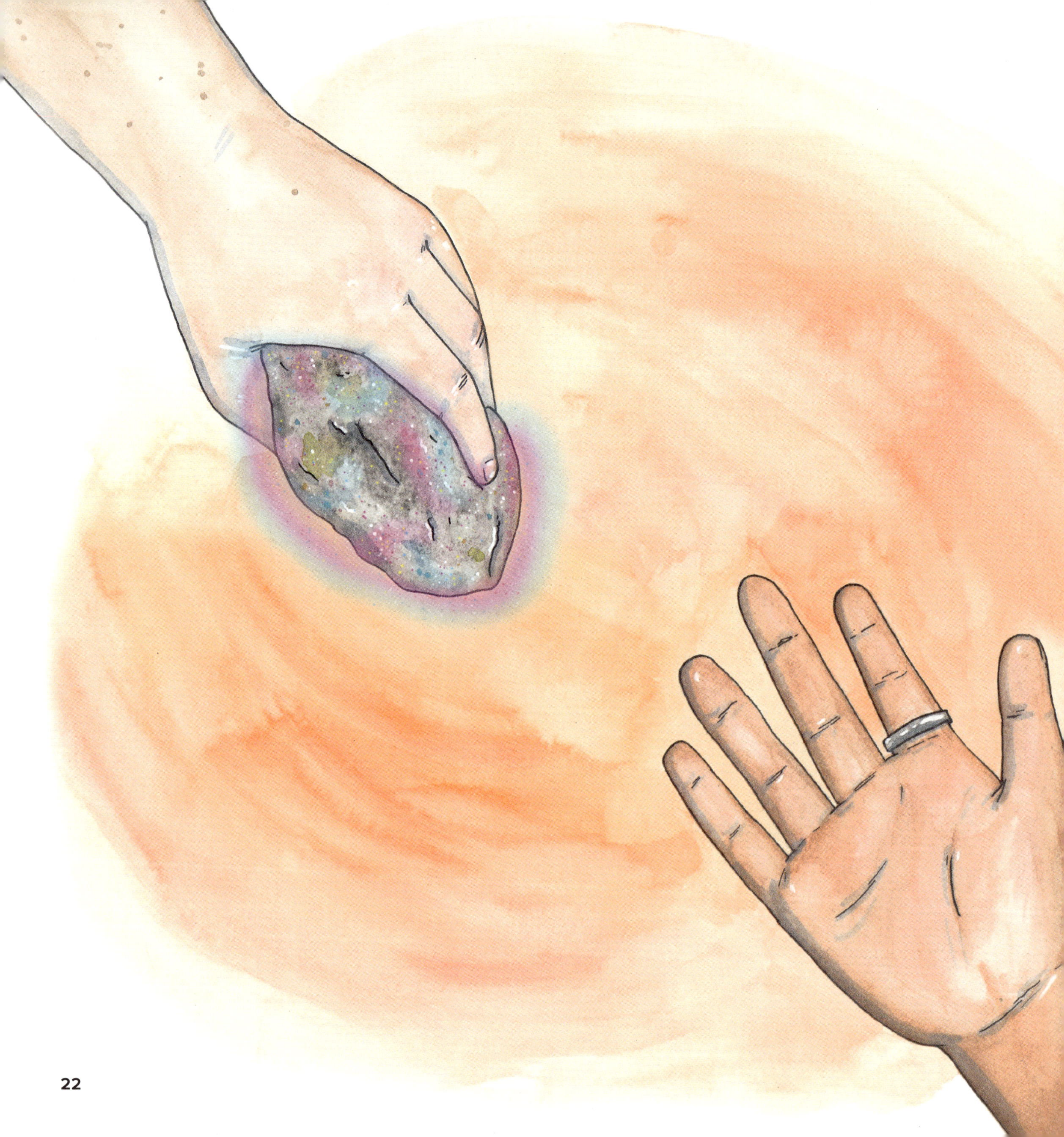

Lani smiles.

After the soccer game, Lani's friends come over to share cookies.

"Mama, this day got brighter when everybody helped each other."
"It sure did!" Mama hugs Lani.
"I'm glad Tai is here. I know what I'm going to do."

NOTE FROM THE AUTHOR

I believe that every child and every person on earth has gifts to share.

As a therapist who works with children, I begin by encouraging them to identify their own strengths and gifts. Next, I introduce the concept that each one of us has some skills or practices that we find more difficult than others, and there is no shame in that. It's part of being human. Together, we identify some areas that are difficult for them, and these become our therapeutic goals for growth.

When children discover their ability to help others by using their own personal strengths and inner gifts, it builds their confidence. It enables them to see opportunities to share their gifts with their community and in their world. Likewise, when children learn that it's okay to accept help in areas that are more difficult for them, it creates space for growth.

As a community, our gifts and struggles fit together like a puzzle. When I share my gifts and strengths with you, and you share your gifts and strengths with me, our gifts and struggles fit together like a puzzle. I wrote *The Helping Rock* to share this amazing concept with children.

Adults can emphasize this lesson by normalizing the concept of struggles and gifts. When children struggle, we can support them with compassion and connection and then gently show them that growth is possible. By doing this, we create an environment for children where mistakes are okay, a mindset of learning and growing is embraced, and help is seen as something to be grateful for.

When we share our gifts with others, and when we receive the help that others offer to us, together, we are stronger. Sharing our gifts makes the world a brighter, more welcoming place.

Tanya Hoover, MSW, RSW, CPT

CURIOUS QUESTIONS

The Helping Rock presents opportunities to talk with children about giving and receiving help. When asking questions, consider the child's age and focus on themes that match their understanding. Here are a few questions to help you get started:

- In the story, Mama says we all need help once in a while. What have you needed help with? Who has helped you?
- In the story, Mama says we all have gifts. What does she mean? What are your gifts?
- Paco helps Lani by staying close when she feels sad and frustrated. Who stays close to you when you feel sad or frustrated? How does it feel to have a pet or loved one stay with you through difficult times?
- Lani has a health condition that makes it harder for her to keep her balance. This is why she wears a brace on her leg called an ankle-foot orthosis (AFO). She says she's the last one to learn how to ride a bike. Have you ever felt like everybody else could do something that was hard for you? How did you get through that challenge?
- The story ends with Lani saying that she knows what she wants to do. What do you think she does? Look at the illustrations for clues.
- Can you name all the ways that people are helping each other in the story? Now look at the illustrations and see if you can find more examples of people helping each other.

ACTIVITIES

Many children like to communicate through activities. Consider including the following activities as you look through the book with a young reader.

Share Your Gifts

Supplies needed:

- Rocks
- Permanent markers
- Basket

Start by brainstorming together different gifts and ways of helping. Look through the text and illustrations in *The Helping Rock* to find examples. What other ideas can you think of? The possibilities for helping and sharing our gifts are endless. Every idea counts!

Next, take five rocks. On each rock, write one word to represent a gift you have to share. Put your rocks in the basket as a reminder of these gifts, and look for opportunities to share your gifts. You may even want to give a rock to someone when you do, just like Lani and her friends!

Why do you think it's important to share our gifts? How does sharing our gifts make our communities stronger? How does it feel when you think about sharing your gifts with others?

The Power of *Yet*

Add a second part to the above activity by thinking about something you want to do but aren't able to *yet*. Adding the word *yet* is a reminder that although you may not be able to do something right now, you can grow by learning how.

On two rocks, write down something that feels hard for you, that you can't do yet, or that you would like help with. Put these goals in a second basket.

What are some things you can do to practice or learn this skill? Is there someone who can help you? When someone helps you, they are sharing their gifts with you. How does it feel to let others share their gifts with you?

Free Resources

Additional resources promoting the concepts in *The Helping Rock* are available as downloadable PDFs in the Free Resources section of our website (www.ctrinstitute.com):

- Printable coloring pages with images from the book
- Printable finger puppets depicting the book's characters that children can color and assemble
- A more detailed workbook that includes additional questions and activities

TANYA HOOVER

Author

Tanya works as a Play Therapist in Winnipeg, Manitoba, Canada. She loves supporting children as they find their gifts and learn to value the help they receive along the way. Tanya's favorite way to play is by exploring nature with her family: cross-country skiing in winter, and camping and swimming in Manitoba's lakes in summer. Tanya lives with her two children, her husband, and her two snuggly and playful cats, Cinnamon and Holly. This is Tanya's first published book.

SHANNON O'TOOLE

Illustrator

Shannon is a painter, children's book illustrator, and an elementary school teacher living outside of Toronto, Ontario, Canada. She loves exploring new ways to tell stories through her art. Shannon's artistic practices are inspired by the many unique characters and people in her life. When she is not painting, Shannon enjoys watching classic movies and exploring new recipes to cook. This is the 12th children's book she's illustrated.

PACO

Meet Paco, the inspiration for the dog in this story. Paco lives on a farm with Tanya's sister and her family. He likes to follow his people around their farm, jump in the pond to fetch sticks in summer, and chase hockey pucks on the icy pond in winter. Paco is a friendly and loyal dog who has helped people get over their fear of dogs. Before meeting Paco, Tanya's son was nervous about dogs. After spending a day with Paco on his farm, Tanya's son said he loves dogs and would like to have a blue heeler one day.

ABOUT THE CRISIS & TRAUMA RESOURCE INSTITUTE (CTRI)

CTRI's mission is to inspire learning and improve lives. We are a leading provider of professional development training and resources in the areas of mental health and counseling skills.

For more information:

www.ctrinstitute.com
info@ctrinstitute.com
877-353-3205